Unexpected Savior

AN INDUCTIVE BIBLE STUDY
ON THE GOSPEL OF MARK

By
Erin H. Warren

feasting on truth

Copyright © 2023 by Erin H. Warren
Published by Headley Warren Productions LLC
Orlando, Florida
www.FeastingOnTruth.com

ISBN 978-1-959305-10-1

contents

start here

We have all faced unexpected news. We were expecting one thing, but something else happened. Our minds may immediately go to something negative: the unexpected diagnosis, the unexpected betrayal, the unexpected letdown. But unexpected does not necessarily mean bad news. *Merriam-Webster Dictionary* defines *unexpected* as "unforeseen."[1] It's something we simply did not see coming.

The Old Testament is full of prophecies about the coming Messiah. Woven into the fabric of the Jewish faith is the anticipation of a Deliverer. They were expecting a Savior. You might look at the title of the Bible study and think, *Wait. They did expect a Savior.* True. The people of God were hoping for a military savior, one who would defeat the Roman empire and re-establish the kingdom of God in the Promised Land of Israel.

But Jesus came to do so much more than save them from Rome.

As Christianity spread and the early church grew, believers from both Jewish and Gentile backgrounds came together in one beautifully diverse family of God. But persecution increased too. Inevitably, some began to question their faith. Was following Jesus worth all the hardship here on earth?

But Jesus came to give us so much more than a "good life" here.

Today, we can still lose sight of who Jesus is and what He came to accomplish. We fall into the trap of thinking Jesus did us this huge favor by dying in our place and giving us a "get-out-of-hell-free" card. We allow the cover of grace to enable our sin. Sometimes we approach Jesus as a genie, waiting to grant our every wish, wanting what we can get from Jesus more than we want Jesus Himself.

But Jesus came to do so much more than save us from hell and grant our wishes.

That is the theme of the Gospel of Mark. Jesus was not what they were expecting; He was better.

A LITTLE BACKGROUND INFORMATION

Most scholars believe the Gospel of Mark was written by John Mark, the cousin of Barnabas (see Acts 12–15), in the mid 50s to late 60s AD. Because of the themes of suffering throughout

---

1   "Unexpected." *Merriam-Webster.com Dictionary*, Merriam-Webster, https://www.merriam-webster.com/dictionary/unexpected. Accessed 15 Aug. 2023.

the book, most believe it was written after 64 AD, during the intense persecution of the church under Nero. Mark is the shortest gospel (written to fit on one scroll) and probably the earliest recorded account of the life of Jesus.

Mark had a close relationship with the apostle Peter (1 Peter 5:13), who was an eyewitness to these events and most likely Mark's source. The gospel was written to a primarily Gentile (non-Jewish) audience, and contains fewer Old Testament references than the other gospels.

As I began studying Scripture inductively, I learned something fascinating about the gospels: they are not necessarily written in chronological order. The authors strategically and beautifully order stories to reinforce key ideas and themes about who Jesus is, and I have been amazed at the masterful structure within Mark's words (which may very well recount Peter's preaching; see Acts 10:34–43).

> *Although the style of Mark approximates everyday spoken Greek rather than affecting high literary quality, the Gospel nevertheless displays considerable sophistication in literary intention and design, as is evinced by Mark's sandwich technique, use of irony, and special motifs of insiders-outsiders, command to silence, and the journey. These and other literary conventions are employed by the author of the Second Gospel in order to portray a profoundly theological conception of Jesus as the authoritative yet suffering Son of God.[1]*
> —James R. Edwards

Mark's words may have been simple, but his structure most certainly is not. As we study, pay attention to these juxtapositions that lead us to the meaning therein. At first glance, Mark appears to be a fly-by, fast-hitting retelling of the story of Jesus. But as we slow down and look deeper, we will see incredible depth that points us to the authority, mission and accomplishment of Jesus, God the Son.

The book is often separated into three sections, each with its own focus and taking place in its own location:

- Mark 1–8:26: The Authority of Jesus; Location: around Galilee
- Mark 8:27–10: The Mission of Jesus; Location: on the road to Jerusalem
- Mark 11–16: The Accomplishment of Jesus; Location: in and around Jerusalem

Mark repeatedly mentions the human emotion of Jesus, but I like to think of it more as divine grief. In Isaiah, the coming Messiah is prophesied to be a "man of sorrows" and familiar with grief and pain:

> *Who has believed what he has heard from us?*
> *And to whom has the arm of the LORD been revealed?*
> *For he grew up before him like a young plant,*
> *and like a root out of dry ground;*
> *he had no form or majesty that we should look at him,*

---

1   Edwards, James R.. *The Pillar New Testament Commentary / The Gospel According to Mark*, Eerdmans, Grand Rapids, Mich, 2002. Page 3.

and no beauty that we should desire him.
He was despised and rejected by men,
   a man of sorrows and acquainted with grief;
and as one from whom men hide their faces
   he was despised, and we esteemed him not.
Isaiah 53:1–3

Jesus was acquainted with grief. He mourned the brokenness around Him. He grew angry at the sin of those who led His sheep astray. He was the suffering servant, the One who came not to be served, but to serve. He gave His life as a ransom for many, constraining Himself to human skin, shedding His own blood, so that we might be able to dwell with the presence of God both now and for eternity.

Have this mind among yourselves, which is yours in Christ Jesus, who, though
he was in the form of God, did not count equality with God a thing to be
grasped, but emptied himself, by taking the form of a servant, being born in
the likeness of men. And being found in human form, he humbled himself by
becoming obedient to the point of death, even death on a cross.
Philippians 2:5–8

Jesus was not a conquering king, but rather a man of sorrows and a servant. He was the unexpected Savior.

As you go through this study, keep this context top of mind. Remember, we have the full story and the entire canon of Scripture. The disciples were learning in real-time the truth of who Jesus is and what He came to accomplish.

WHY STUDY INDUCTIVELY?

This study is designed to provide a foundation for inductive Bible study. When I first heard of inductive study, I was pretty intimidated. But, it's just a fancy term for studying with your own heart and mind first. I honestly didn't even know I *could* study this way until a few years ago at a conference. I had the privilege of hearing one of my favorite Bible teachers speak, and the following quote from her talk forever changed the way I look at Bible study:

We cannot be content being curators of other people's opinions about a book we
can't be bothered to read ourselves. — Jen Wilkin

I realized my entire Christian life I had been a librarian, curating other people's thoughts and beliefs and study findings. It became my driving passion to not only read and study Scripture for myself, but to help other women do the same. I'm so glad you're here! My prayer is that this book helps you:

- Release the bonds of a "perfect quiet time" to find deeper, richer time in the Word

- Build confidence as you learn how to study the Bible firsthand

7

- Discover truths about God and His character
- Connect the Old and New Testaments
- Grow in your faith and knowledge in a way that produces life change

HOW TO USE THIS STUDY

Feasting on Truth has several levels of studies, and I classify this one as True Inductive. We will use four simple questions (see page 11) to guide our study. Each week will focus on one chapter, and you'll see that the homework includes a guide through those four questions. Under *What Does This Mean?* you'll see some suggested words to look up in the dictionary as well as space to write cross-references (other verses that speak to the same topic or help explain the meaning). There are also a few questions to help kick-start your study but won't cover everything. These are intended to help get you thinking on your own and are not all-inclusive of the meaning. For this study, the questions will also help you see the larger picture and juxtaposition of stories. I purposely left this section wide open for you, or rather for the Holy Spirit. I want you to have the freedom to take notes in the format you choose: write out specific verses, record observations, make a chart, rewrite commentary quotes or Greek definitions, etc. Each week also includes pages for teaching notes and group notes. I know it can sound intimidating, but I also know you can do it!

Studying a chapter a week is my favorite way to study. I encourage you to read each chapter (and listen to it on your favorite Bible app) over and over throughout the week, then pick a day or two to focus on studying. Always, always start with prayer. Ask the Holy Spirit to guide you in your study time and to reveal truth to you. It's His job (John 14:26; 16:13–15). You'll be amazed at what the Holy Spirit can teach when you give Him the space to speak.

Teaching for each chapter is available on Season 10 of the Feasting on Truth Podcast or my YouTube channel: www.FeastingOnTruth.com/c/erinhwarren.

Here are some more tips to help you as you study:

Move Slowly
Many Bible studies plow through Scripture, covering a chapter (or sometimes more) a day. There's certainly a time and a place for that, but I've found when I move through Scripture slowly, reading small sections or focusing on one aspect of the study over the course of one week, the Word of God soaks into my heart and mind deeply. I remember it more easily. I memorize it more effectively. What I love about this particular way of studying is that if I feel the need to stop and let a particular verse sink in, I can do so without feeling like I'm falling behind. It also leaves room for the Holy Spirit to do what only He can do. Which leads me to . . .

Let the Holy Spirit Guide You
Jesus gives us this promise in John 14:26: "But the Helper, the Holy Spirit, whom the Father will send in my name, he will teach you all things and bring to your remembrance all that I have said to you." Anytime I sit down to study, I start with prayer. I ask the Holy Spirit to teach me all the things and to help me remember all the things. That's His job. He's there to help, so invite Him into your time.

Take the Pressure Off
Our time with the Lord doesn't have to be this picture-perfect composition of Bible, notebook, and a cup of coffee (oh how I do love me some good coffee though). The words "quiet time" are

8

not in the Bible, and I've found one size does not fit all. Our time in the Word will change with our stage of life. I tend to deep-dive study about twice a week, but I meditate on it every day. You may sit down and do all of your study in one day or you may devote an hour a day. Find what works for you and stick with it!

Don't Do This Alone

Some of my deepest relationships are ones built on the Word. They are women who gathered around a table or in a living room or online, and we had hard conversations with the Word of Truth between us. Invite a few girlfriends to do this with you. I even included a fun recipe in the back of the book you can make when you get together!

I recommend completing all of the homework on your own before listening to the teaching for the week. You can either listen on your own time or watch together with your group.

Finding time is hard. Women often tell me that they need to put their families first, that work is too crazy, or that they just don't have time to get together with other women for Bible study. Can I challenge you a bit? Is there any time more well spent than investing in our relationship with God? It's hard to pour out from an empty cup. We need to be constantly filled with Jesus, so we can pour out Jesus to our friends, family, and to God. Yes, this may look different in different seasons of life, but you won't regret making it a priority to spend time in the Word with other women.

COMPANION TEACHINGS AND OTHER RESOURCES

I am committed to walking alongside you as you study Scripture inductively. I know you can do this, and I want to help you be successful. I have personally curated and put together a valuable study resource for you called *The Alongside Guide*. Each week, you'll receive an email from me with helpful insight, links to that week's teaching video and podcast, study notes with cross-references, quotes, characteristics of God, small group discussion questions, and more. It's everything you need to be successful in your study, and it gets delivered right to your inbox. Scan the QR code or visit FeastingOnTruth.com/Mark to sign up.

LET'S FEAST

The word *feast* is rooted in abundance, and that's what awaits us in Scripture: a table laid out before us, not only for our essential nourishment, but also for our enjoyment. It is my prayer that through this study of Mark, you will gain a clearer picture of who Jesus is and what He came to do. I pray that the Holy Spirit meets you in the pages of this gospel and teaches you about this man of sorrows, suffering servant, and unexpected Savior. And in turn, I pray that it emboldens your faith as you follow Him, carrying your cross, overcoming areas of unbelief, and setting your mind on the things of God.

I am cheering for you! Happy feasting!

Because of Christ,

Erin H. Warren

four simple questions

Good Bible study is rooted in asking the right questions of Scripture. Our first inclination in Bible study is often to ask, "What does this mean to me?" We want to cut right to the ending. Instead, learning to first understand the context, summary, and character of God in the passage will help us better discern the meaning and our response. I have adopted what I call *Four Simple Questions* as the foundation of my time in the Word. Yes, this takes a little more time and effort, but the practice of persevering through the Word is a valuable one. These four simple questions, as well as other helpful tips and resources for inductive study, are further explained in my book, *Feasting on Truth: Savor the Life-giving Word of God.*

START WITH CONTEXT

It's important to remember that while the Bible was written for us and is applicable to our lives today (Hebrews 4:12), we are not the original audience. It is a book not written in modern America, but in the ancient Middle East. If we do not first answer some key questions to understand the context, we cannot properly understand the passage and its intent. Most of these answers can be found in a good study Bible.

FOUR SIMPLE QUESTIONS

I realized that one of my downfalls when attempting to read and study the Bible for myself was not knowing which questions to ask. Many of the methods I tried were either too open or too rigid. Asking four simple questions provided the right balance of structure and flexibility I needed. I want to release you from thinking this has to look a certain way—it doesn't. Basically: Are you showing up? Are you changing? Are you connected? Does that make you want to keep showing up? If you answer yes to all of these, then you're on the right track! Here is a brief overview of each question:

11

1. **What does this say?**
   Before we can interpret Scripture, we need to know what's going on in the passage. Some methods would call this *observation* or the *aim of the passage*.

   - Write a 1–2 sentence summary of what the passage is about—no interpretation, just the facts.

   - Answer the questions: Who? What? Where? When?

   - Are there any repeated words or phrases?

   - Are there any transitional words (therefore, so, but, and, etc.)? Remember, every word is there for a reason.

2. **What does this say about God?**
   This to me has been the most transformative question to ask during Bible study. This book is not about us; it's about God. His character and name are written on every page. Before we can understand our response, we must know who He is.

   - What names of God are used? (His names speak to His character.)

   - What characteristics of God are in this passage?

   - I include Jesus in this as well: What does this passage tell us about Jesus?

   - You can find lists of the names and characteristics of God on pages 18–19.

   - Each week, complete the sentence "Because God is _____, I can _____."

3. **What does this mean?**
   PRAY. PRAY. PRAY. Ask the Holy Spirit to guide you in this. Using context, the summary, and other observations you have made, begin to be a detective. Remember the lens through which you are looking. Yes, this takes work, but it's worth doing!

   - Read the passage in multiple translations. What differences do you see?

   - Look up words in the English dictionary.

   - What other passages in Scripture are related to this one? (These are called cross-references.)

   - Read a trusted commentary or study Bible.

   - Research the original language (the Old Testament was originally written in Hebrew and the New Testament in Greek).

   - Go to FeastingOnTruth.com/Resources for recommended resources, Bibles, and commentaries.

4. **How should I respond?**
   Our Bible study should change us. John 17:17 says, "Sanctify them in the truth; your word is truth." *Sanctify* is a big churchy word that means "to purify or to make holy." It's the act of separating ourselves from the actions of our flesh and dedicating more of our lives and actions to God. God's Word has a purpose in our lives (Isaiah 55:10–11), and we shouldn't stop at knowing its meaning. Instead, we should respond:

   - Is there an action I need to take?

12

- A conversation I need to have?
- A moment of worship?
- Something I should let go?
- Write out a prayer.

However you feel led to respond, write it down and enlist someone to hold you accountable.

OTHER HELPFUL TIPS

Listen to the Passage

Use a Bible app to listen to the passages each week. We often feel like this is a cop-out, but for thousands of years, the Word of God was passed down orally from generation to generation. It's a book meant to be read out loud, and when you listen to it, you'll be amazed at how much you pick up on that you didn't notice when reading it.

Use Different Colored Pens

I've found using different colored pens when writing my study notes helps me remember where the note came from. For instance, I use different colors for rewriting the Scripture verses, my thoughts, certain study Bibles, cross-references or different translations, commentary quotes, and Greek or Hebrew word definitions. I don't really have a color system, so the colors change from time to time. That's okay too!

Start with a Clean Copy of God's Word

A study Bible adds additional commentary. Using a Bible that doesn't have any additional commentary removes the temptation to peek at notes before fully understanding the passage on your own. If you do not have a non-study Bible, don't fret! You can print out chapters on several Bible websites including www.BibleGateway.com. I use an ESV journaling Bible for my initial study (which has very few footnotes), then move to other translations and other study Bibles as I go through my study week. Speaking of translations . . .

A Note About Translations

There are a myriad of translations out there, so how do you know which to pick? First, it's important to know where translations come from. The Old Testament was originally written in Hebrew, while the New Testament was written in Greek (though a few portions of Scripture were written in Aramaic).

Over the years, translators have used original copies written in these languages to interpret Scripture into English (and other languages as well). Translations fall on a spectrum between two ends: word-for-word (translations that use the closest English word to the original word) and thought-for-thought (translations that rephrase the words into more modern, understandable English). Technically, all of them are a mix of the two, but some lean more toward one end or the other.

Some examples of translations that lean toward word-for-word include: English Standard Version (ESV—my top choice), New American Standard Bible (NAS or NASB), and King James Version (KJV). These are the closest to the original language, but we can sometimes miss the cultural context.

An example of thought-for-thought is the New Living Translation (NLT).

There are also versions that are more toward the middle of the spectrum, such as the Christian Standard Bible (CSB) and the New International Version (NIV).

The last kind of translation is not necessarily a translation at all, but rather a paraphrase. Paraphrase Bibles, like *The Message*, should be treated more like commentary because, while they can bring insight into the meaning of the passage, they are not Scripture themselves. I rarely use this type. If you do use a paraphrase, wait until you've completed questions 1–3 and are consulting other commentaries for additional insights.

Welcome to the Feast!

See? Simple. Yes, it takes practice, but honestly, it doesn't take as long as you'd think. You just have to be willing to spend time with Jesus. In Acts 4, Peter and John are on trial before the religious leaders (the smartest of the smart when it came to the Law), and in verse 13 it says, "Now when they saw the boldness of Peter and John, and perceived that they were uneducated, common men, they were astonished. And they recognized that they had been with Jesus." Uneducated. Common. Peter and John hadn't been to seminary, but they had been *with* Jesus.

What I've found is that there is not one method that will make all of this work for you. The power is not in the method. The power is in the Word of God. The power is in spending time with Jesus in the Word with the Holy Spirit as your guide.

When you see your life change and you find community around the Word, you will find yourself returning to Scripture, growing more confident as you study, and discovering the joy and excitement of Feasting on Truth.

Visit FeastingOnTruth.com/HowTo for more information
and in-depth teachings on these questions.

small group guide

I am a firm believer in gathering together around the Word of God. It is at the heart of Feasting on Truth. As stated in *start here*, I believe that small group discussion is incredibly important when studying the Bible. I heard a pastor say, "Our time in the Word should be personal but never private." I do not believe we are called to study in isolation, I believe it is in places of isolation where Satan loves to tempt us. Discussing the passage in a small group setting (even if it's with only one other woman) helps confirm what the Holy Spirit taught us. It holds us accountable to truth. Not only that, but I learn so much from other women too. They will see truths within those passages that I miss. It helps build layers of understanding.

Leading a group is not nearly as difficult as it seems. I like to think of group leaders more like discussion leaders. A great discussion leader talks less than a third of the group time. You may need to speak first or jump in to get the conversation going, but the goal is to get the group talking.

Teaching for each chapter is available on Season 10 of the Feasting on Truth podcast or my YouTube channel: YouTube.com/c/erinhwarren.

Here are some other tips and a guide for your small group time:

Lead with authenticity
You do not have to have all the answers or have it all together to lead. I do not have it all together, and I fail miserably every day at doing what I know I should (Romans 7!). But I don't have to air all my dirty laundry to be authentic, and I never want my authenticity to enable sin in other people's lives. I've found that when I'm real about where I am and I invite women in to see how God is working on me in those areas, it invites them into authentic life change as well.

Set up a group text or use a group chat app
Connection throughout the week is key to building connection within your group. If you are not tech savvy or keeping up with a group chat isn't your strength, ask someone in the group to take charge of that. It's a great way to get others involved too! Throughout the week, you can check in on your group or share a verse or a particular insight into the passage.

Start with an ice breaker question
It doesn't have to be deep or spiritual, just something to get the conversation flowing. These types of questions are always a great way to help a group of women get to know each other.

15

Share your summary

Have the women share their summary for that week's passage. Depending on the size of your group, you may want to limit this to two to three women.

Ask: What characteristics of God did you see in this week's passage?

This works well "popcorn style." Let the women jump in with various names and characteristics of God and the verses that correspond. I usually add these to my own notes as well.

Use the weekly discussion questions

There are discussion questions marked within each week's homework. For additional weekly discussion questions, go to FeastingOnTruth.com/Mark and sign up to receive *The Alongside Guide* in your email. Each week, you'll get additional questions (as well as other resources and notes) delivered right to your inbox.

Share "Because God is" statements

This is a simple one, and I love it when everyone shares theirs! Depending on how long you have been together, some women in your group may not feel comfortable sharing the nitty-gritty of their lives. Having everyone share their "Because God is" statement is a way to engage the women who do not feel comfortable speaking up.

Share prayer requests

Sharing what is going on in our lives opens the door to build community and meet needs. I'll never forget sitting in a group when a woman shared that she needed prayer that she could pass her driving test. Across the table, another woman in the group spoke up and said, "I can help you learn to drive!" A couple months later, I received a picture of the two women holding a brand-new driver's license. It was incredible! Praying for one another is commanded, so allow time for this with your group. Pray with one another. Pray throughout the week. When we do this, we get to share an inheritance in what God is doing through the lives of others.

GROUP LIST

NAME	PHONE	EMAIL

knowing God

For too many years, I struggled with knowing how to interpret Scripture and apply these ancient words to my life. I did not know that God promises to equip us in studying Scripture through the Holy Spirit. And truthfully, I treated my Bible like one of those balls you shake, ask a question, flip over, and find your answer. Too many times I came to Scripture looking for an answer to my question, or I treated it like a yearbook—looking for all the pictures of myself.

Then, I began asking a different question, and my entire Bible study and life changed. I asked, "What does this say about God?" This shifted my perspective from a self-centered approach toward Scripture (where I am always asking, "What does this mean *to* me or *for* me?") to a God-centered approach—intentionally looking for and seeking out what each passage teaches me about God.

The Bible is not about me. It is first and foremost a book about God, and His name and character are written across every page. Our purpose on earth is to know God and make Him known, to love God and love others. But we can't love what we don't know; we can't worship what we don't know. And the primary way we know God is through His Word. The pursuit of knowledge about God is not optional; it's essential.

On the following pages, you will find two lists to help you: Names of God and Characteristics of God. It's not comprehensive, and there are spaces for you to add others as you discover more with each passage you read. Here are ways you can have a God-centered approach to your study:

- Ask, "What characteristics of God do I see in this passage?"
- Ask, "What names of God do I see in this passage?" (His names speak to His character.)
- Complete this sentence: Because God is _____, I can _____.

While there are different roles within the Trinity (God the Father, God the Son, God the Holy Spirit), for the sake of simplicity, I study them as One. Our tendency when studying the gospels is to focus solely on the character of Jesus. But Jesus is God. In your weekly study, the characteristics of God are also the characteristics of Jesus, and your response in light of God's character is also your response in light of Jesus' character. If you need further help, visit www.FeastingOnTruth.com for more information and resources.

names of God

Abba Father

Adonai *(Lord, Master)*

Alpha and Omega

Bread of Life

Chief Cornerstone

Creator

Deliverer

El Elyon *(The Most High God)*

El Olam *(The Everlasting God)*

El Roi *(The God Who Sees Me)*

El Shaddai *(The Lord God Almighty)*

Elohim

Emmanuel

Everlasting Father

Great High Priest

Holy One

I AM

King of Kings

Lamb of God

Light of the World

Lion of Judah

Lord of Lords

Mighty God

Morning Star

Prince of Peace

Resurrection and the Life

Savior

Wonderful Counselor

Yahweh Amen *(The Lord is Truth)*

Yahweh Jireh *(The Lord Provides)*

Yahweh Nissi *(The Lord is my Banner)*

Yahweh-Raah *(The Lord is my Shepherd)*

Yahweh Rapha *(The Lord Heals)*

Yahweh Shalom *(The Lord is Peace)*

characteristics of God

Abounding in Steadfast Love

Compassionate

Deliberate

Faithful

Forgiving

Full of Grace

Good

Glorious

Gracious

Guide

Holy

Immutable *(Unchanging)*

Infinite

Invisible

Jealous

Just

Kind

Long-Suffering/Patient

Love

Merciful

Mighty

Omnipotent *(All-Powerful)*

Omnipresent

Omniscient *(All-Knowing)*

One

Perfect

Protector

Provider

Refuge/Help

Righteous

Self-Sufficient

Slow to Anger

Sovereign

Trustworthy

Truth

Wise

With Us

19

Unexpected Savior

KNOWING GOD NOTES

Unexpected Savior

MAPS

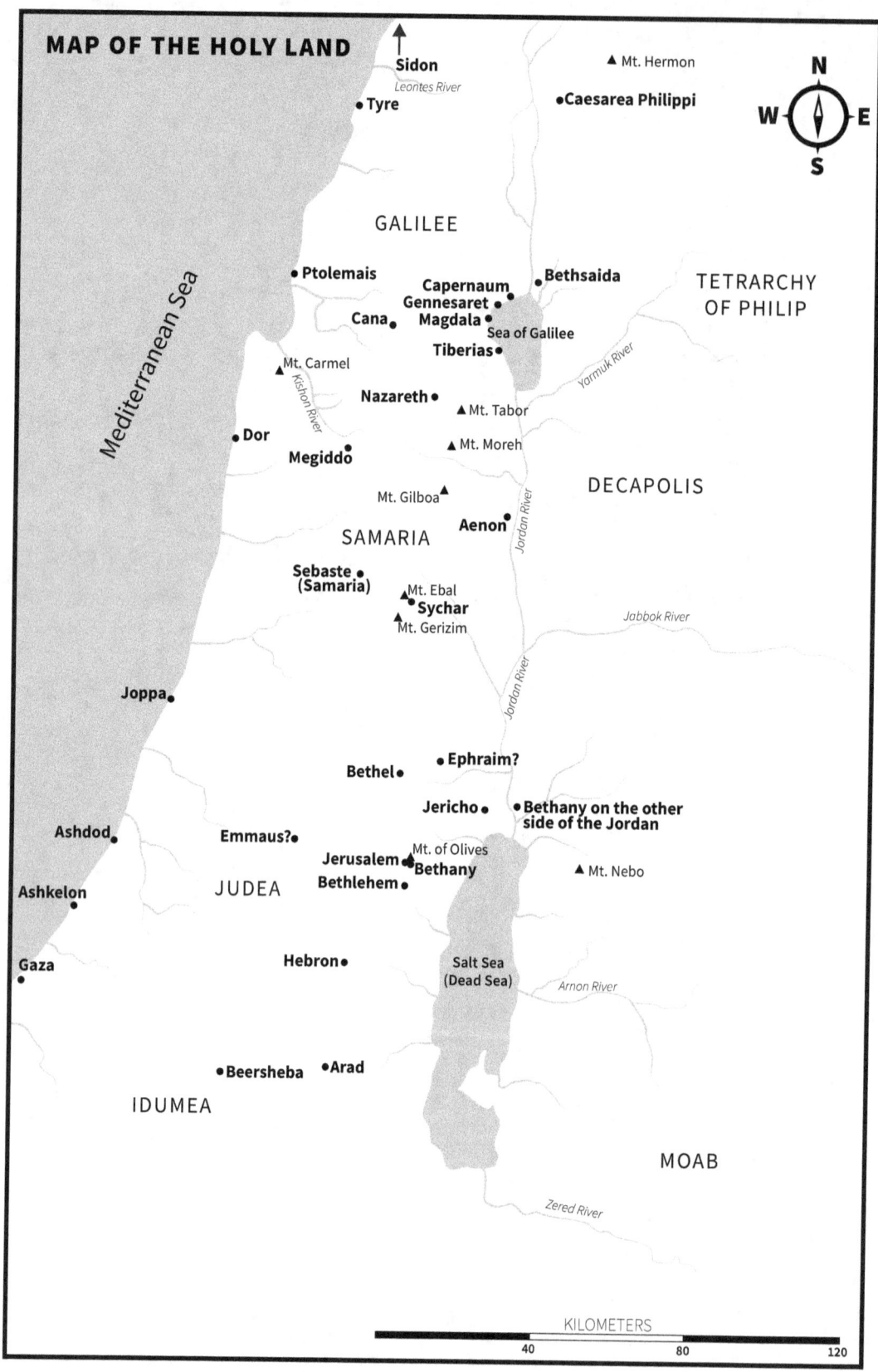

MAP OF THE HOLY LAND

Sidon
Leontes River
Tyre
Mt. Hermon
Caesarea Philippi

N
W E
S

GALILEE

Mediterranean Sea

Ptolemais
Capernaum
Gennesaret
Cana
Magdala
Tiberias
Bethsaida
Sea of Galilee

TETRARCHY
OF PHILIP

Mt. Carmel
Kishon River
Nazareth
Mt. Tabor
Yarmuk River

Dor
Megiddo
Mt. Moreh
DECAPOLIS

Mt. Gilboa
Aenon
Jordan River

SAMARIA

Sebaste
(Samaria)
Mt. Ebal
Sychar
Mt. Gerizim
Jabbok River

Jordan River

Joppa

Ephraim?
Bethel
Jericho
Bethany on the other
side of the Jordan

Ashdod
Emmaus?
Mt. of Olives
Jerusalem Bethany
Bethlehem
Mt. Nebo

Ashkelon

JUDEA

Gaza

Hebron
Salt Sea
(Dead Sea)
Arnon River

Beersheba Arad

IDUMEA

MOAB

Zered River

KILOMETERS
40   80   120

22

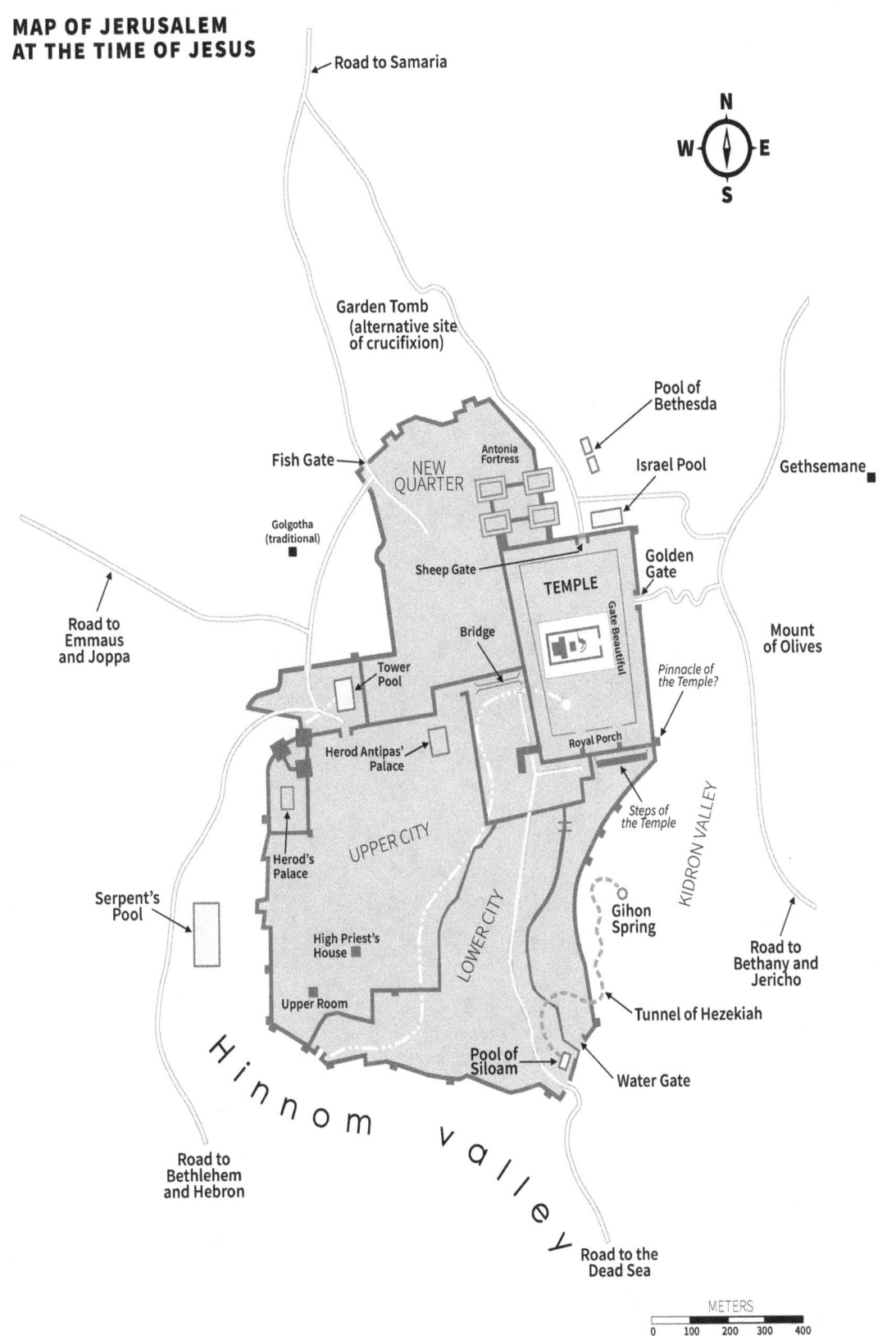

MAP OF JERUSALEM AT THE TIME OF JESUS

Road to Samaria

N W E S

Garden Tomb (alternative site of crucifixion)

Pool of Bethesda

Fish Gate

NEW QUARTER

Antonia Fortress

Israel Pool

Gethsemane

Golgotha (traditional)

Sheep Gate

TEMPLE

Golden Gate

Road to Emmaus and Joppa

Tower Pool

Bridge

Gate Beautiful

Mount of Olives

Pinnacle of the Temple?

Herod Antipas' Palace

Royal Porch

Steps of the Temple

KIDRON VALLEY

UPPER CITY

Herod's Palace

Serpent's Pool

Gihon Spring

LOWER CITY

Road to Bethany and Jericho

High Priest's House

Tunnel of Hezekiah

Upper Room

Pool of Siloam

Water Gate

Hinnom valley

Road to Bethlehem and Hebron

Road to the Dead Sea

METERS
0   100   200   300   400

23

Unexpected Savior

CONTEXT

Unexpected
Savior

CONTEXT NOTES

Who wrote the book of Mark?

What do you know about this author?

To whom was this book written?

When was it written?

What is the genre of this book?

What was the intent or purpose?

What was going on in history when it was written?

Unexpected Savior

CONTEXT NOTES

Unexpected Savior

CONTEXT NOTES

Unexpected
Savior

TEACHING NOTES

Unexpected Savior

TEACHING NOTES

Unexpected Savior

GROUP NOTES

Unexpected Savior

GROUP NOTES

Unexpected Savior

MARK 1

Unexpected Savior

READ MARK 1

WHAT DOES THIS SAY?

Write a 2–3 sentence summary of this passage.

Who? What? Where? When?

List any repeated words or phrases.

List any transitional words.

WHAT DOES THIS SAY ABOUT GOD?

What characteristics of God do you see in this passage?

WHAT DOES THIS MEAN?

Look up the following words in the dictionary and write out their definitions:

Fulfilled:

Authority:

_____:

_____:

Unexpected Savior

CROSS-REFERENCES

Acts 1:5:

Galatians 4:1–7:

_____:

_____:

_____:

STARTER QUESTIONS

How does Mark show Jesus as a Man of Sorrows, Servant, or Savior in this passage?

In this chapter, what does Mark show that Jesus has authority over?

DISCUSSION: Read the following Old Testament verses in context. What prophecies do you see fulfilled in Mark 1?

Malachi 2:17–3:3:

Unexpected Savior

Isaiah 40:3:

Isaiah 44:1–5:

Joel 2:28–32:

Ezekiel 39:29:

Read Isaiah 52:7–12. How does this parallel Jesus' declaration in v. 15?

What do the demons know and declare to be true of Jesus? What does Jesus tell them in response?

DISCUSSION: Why would Jesus not want the truth of who He was declared to the masses?

Unexpected Savior

MARK 1 NOTES

Unexpected Savior

MARK 1 NOTES

HOW SHOULD I RESPOND?

Who is Jesus? What did He come to accomplish?

Write a prayer of thanksgiving for who He is.

Because God is:

    I can:

Unexpected Savior

TEACHING NOTES

Unexpected
Savior

TEACHING NOTES

Unexpected Savior

GROUP NOTES

Unexpected Savior

GROUP NOTES

Unexpected Savior

MARK 2

Unexpected Savior

MARK 2 NOTES

READ MARK 2

WHAT DOES THIS SAY?

Write a 2–3 sentence summary of this passage.

Who? What? Where? When?

List any repeated words or phrases.

List any transitional words.

WHAT DOES THIS SAY ABOUT GOD?

What characteristics of God do you see in this passage?

WHAT DOES THIS MEAN?

Look up the following words in the dictionary and write out their definitions:

Righteous:

Sinner:

Blasphemy:

_____:

CROSS-REFERENCES

Psalm 103:

Colossians 2:16–23:

_____:

_____:

_____:

STARTER QUESTIONS

How does Mark show Jesus as a Man of Sorrows, Servant, or Savior in this passage?

In this chapter, what does Mark show that Jesus has authority over?

DISCUSSION: Jesus draws a comparison here between fasting and a wedding. Read Joel 2:12–16. What is fasting synonymous with? How does this differ from the picture of the wedding?

DISCUSSION: Read Exodus 16 (This is the first place the word *Sabbath* is used in Scripture.) What is the purpose of Sabbath?

Read 1 Samuel 21:1–9 and Leviticus 24:5–9. What insight do you glean about Jesus' response in Mark 2?

DISCUSSION: How does understanding the intent of Sabbath help explain Jesus' response to the Pharisees?

Unexpected
Savior

MARK 2 NOTES

Unexpected Savior

MARK 2 NOTES

HOW SHOULD I RESPOND?

Who is Jesus? What did He come to accomplish?

Write a prayer of thanksgiving for who He is.

Because God is:

    I can:

Unexpected Savior

TEACHING NOTES

Unexpected
Savior

TEACHING NOTES

Unexpected
Savior

GROUP NOTES

Unexpected Savior

GROUP NOTES

Unexpected Savior

MARK 3

READ MARK 3

WHAT DOES THIS SAY?

Write a 2–3 sentence summary of this passage.

Who? What? Where? When?

List any repeated words or phrases.

List any transitional words.

Unexpected
Savior

WHAT DOES THIS SAY ABOUT GOD?

What characteristics of God do you see in this passage?

WHAT DOES THIS MEAN?

Look up the following words in the dictionary and write out their definitions:

Grieved:

Apostles:

_____:

_____:

Unexpected Savior

CROSS-REFERENCES

Exodus 31:12–17:

Romans 8:12–17:

Acts 2:42–47:

_____:

_____:

STARTER QUESTIONS

How does Mark show Jesus as a Man of Sorrows, Servant, or Savior in this passage?

In this chapter, what does Mark show that Jesus has authority over?

How does Mark describe the religious leaders in vv. 1–6? How does Jesus respond to them?

Unexpected
Savior

DISCUSSION: How does this story reiterate the purpose of Sabbath?

DISCUSSION: Who were the twelve apostles? What do you know about these men?

How were the scribes blaspheming the Holy Spirit?

What does Jesus' family say of Jesus?

DISCUSSION: Who does Jesus say is His true family? What does this teach us about the family of God?

Unexpected Savior

MARK 3 NOTES

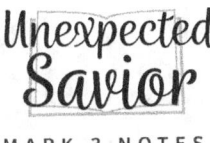

Unexpected Savior

MARK 3 NOTES

HOW SHOULD I RESPOND?

Who is Jesus? What did He come to accomplish?

Write a prayer of thanksgiving for who He is.

Because God is:

    I can:

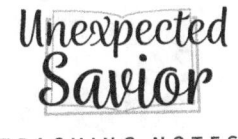

Unexpected Savior

TEACHING NOTES

Unexpected Savior

TEACHING NOTES

Unexpected Savior

GROUP NOTES

Unexpected Savior

GROUP NOTES

Unexpected Savior

MARK 4

READ MARK 4

WHAT DOES THIS SAY?

Write a 2–3 sentence summary of this passage.

Who? What? Where? When?

List any repeated words or phrases.

List any transitional words.

WHAT DOES THIS SAY ABOUT GOD?

What characteristics of God do you see in this passage?

WHAT DOES THIS MEAN?

Look up the following words in the dictionary and write out their definitions:

Parable:

Seed:

_____:

_____:

Unexpected
Savior

MARK 4 NOTES

CROSS-REFERENCES

Isaiah 6:

Isaiah 55:

1 John 2:15–17:

_____:

_____:

STARTER QUESTIONS

How does Mark show Jesus as a Man of Sorrows, Servant, or Savior in this passage?

In this chapter, what does Mark show that Jesus has authority over?

Why does Jesus teach in parables?

Unexpected
Savior

MARK 4 NOTES

WHERE THE SEED FALLS	WHAT HAPPENS TO IT	WHAT IT REPRESENTS

What do these parables teach us about:

God:

The Word:

The Kingdom of God:

DISCUSSION: How do we guard our hearts and minds to remain firmly planted in good soil?

73

What does Jesus do and say to the wind? What happened when He did?

DISCUSSION: How does this reinforce who Jesus is?

What does Jesus say to the disciples? How do they respond?

Unexpected Savior

MARK 4 NOTES

Unexpected Savior

MARK 4 NOTES

Unexpected Savior

MARK 4 NOTES

HOW SHOULD I RESPOND?

Who is Jesus? What did He come to accomplish?

Write a prayer of thanksgiving for who He is.

Because God is:

    I can:

Unexpected Savior

TEACHING NOTES

Unexpected Savior

TEACHING NOTES

Unexpected
Savior

GROUP NOTES

Unexpected Savior

GROUP NOTES

82

Unexpected Savior

MARK 5

Unexpected
Savior

READ MARK 5

WHAT DOES THIS SAY?

Write a 2–3 sentence summary of this passage.

Who? What? Where? When?

List any repeated words or phrases.

List any transitional words.

Unexpected
Savior

WHAT DOES THIS SAY ABOUT GOD?

What characteristics of God do you see in this passage?

WHAT DOES THIS MEAN?

Look up the following words in the dictionary and write out their definitions:

Faith:

Believe:

_____:

_____:

Unexpected Savior

CROSS-REFERENCES

Leviticus 15:19–30:

Hebrews 1:1–4:

_____:

_____:

STARTER QUESTIONS

How does Mark show Jesus as a Man of Sorrows, Servant, or Savior in this passage?

In this chapter, what does Mark show that Jesus has authority over?

In the story of the healing of the demon-possessed man, how do each of these people respond to Jesus:

The demon-possessed man:

The herdsmen and people from the town and country:

The people of the Decapolis:

What was Jairus' job? How does his response to Jesus differ from the other religious leaders we've read about?

How does Mark describe the woman who had an issue of blood?

Read Leviticus 15:19–30. What risk was this woman taking in pressing through the crowd and touching Jesus?

When Jesus asked who touched him, how does the women approach and respond to Jesus? What does Jesus say to her?

DISCUSSION: What does Jesus do for this women by calling her out?

At the home of Jairus, how do the people there respond to Jesus?

Who witnesses the miracle?

DISCUSSION: What does the juxtaposition of these two stories tell us about our awareness of who Jesus is, the power He has, and how should we approach Him?

Unexpected Savior

MARK 5 NOTES

Unexpected Savior

MARK 5 NOTES

90

Unexpected Savior

MARK 5 NOTES

HOW SHOULD I RESPOND?

Who is Jesus? What did He come to accomplish?

Write a prayer of thanksgiving for who He is.

Because God is:

I can:

Unexpected Savior

TEACHING NOTES

Unexpected
Savior

TEACHING NOTES

Unexpected Savior

GROUP NOTES

Unexpected Savior

GROUP NOTES

Unexpected Savior

MARK 6

READ MARK 6

WHAT DOES THIS SAY?

Write a 2–3 sentence summary of this passage.

Who? What? Where? When?

List any repeated words or phrases.

List any transitional words.

Unexpected Savior

WHAT DOES THIS SAY ABOUT GOD?

What characteristics of God do you see in this passage?

WHAT DOES THIS MEAN?

Look up the following words in the dictionary and write out their definitions:

Compassion:

Satisfied:

_____ :

_____ :

CROSS-REFERENCES

Psalm 23:

Acts 18:5–6:

_____:

_____:

STARTER QUESTIONS

How does Mark show Jesus as a Man of Sorrows, Servant, or Savior in this passage?

In this chapter, what does Mark show that Jesus has authority over?

What do the people of Nazareth say of Jesus?

Who do other people think Jesus is?

Unexpected
Savior

MARK 6 NOTES

Who does Herod hope Jesus is?

After the disciples return to Jesus, where does he take them?

How does Jesus describe the crowd who gathers there? How does He respond to them?

What do the people sit on?
DISCUSSION: Write out v. 42. What does this tell us about Jesus?

What happens after they pick up the leftover food?

How did the disciples respond to Jesus? What does this tell us about their understanding of who Jesus is?

DISCUSSION: How does Mark show who Jesus truly is? How does this differ from people's opinions earlier in the chapter?

Unexpected Savior

MARK 6 NOTES

Unexpected Savior

MARK 6 NOTES

Unexpected Savior

MARK 6 NOTES

Unexpected
Savior

HOW SHOULD I RESPOND?

Who is Jesus? What did He come to accomplish?

Write a prayer of thanksgiving for who He is.

Because God is:

    I can:

Unexpected
Savior

TEACHING NOTES

Unexpected Savior

TEACHING NOTES

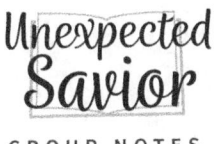

Unexpected Savior

GROUP NOTES

Unexpected
Savior

GROUP NOTES

Unexpected Savior

MARK 7

Unexpected
Savior

READ MARK 7

WHAT DOES THIS SAY?

Write a 2–3 sentence summary of this passage.

Who? What? Where? When?

List any repeated words or phrases.

List any transitional words.

Unexpected Savior

WHAT DOES THIS SAY ABOUT GOD?

What characteristics of God do you see in this passage?

WHAT DOES THIS MEAN?

Look up the following words in the dictionary and write out their definitions:

Tradition:

Defiled:

_____:

_____:

Unexpected Savior

CROSS-REFERENCES

Isaiah 29:13–16:

Romans 8:18–28:

Isaiah 35:

_____:

STARTER QUESTIONS

How does Mark show Jesus as a Man of Sorrows, Servant, or Savior in this passage?

In this chapter, what does Mark show that Jesus has authority over?

What do the Pharisees accuse Jesus' disciples of?

How does Jesus respond to their accusations?

Unexpected
Savior

MARK 7 NOTES

DISCUSSION: What are some ways that we add rules and traditions to God's Word today?

DISCUSSION: What do these verses tell us about the state of our hearts without Jesus?

How does Mark describe the women in v. 26?

What do you know about the view of Gentiles in this day?

DISCUSSION: Compare Jesus' interaction with the Pharisees and the Gentile woman. How does the juxtaposition of these two stories reiterate why Jesus came?

Unexpected
Savior

Where does Jesus go next? Where else in Mark have we seen this location?

What does Jesus do before He heals the deaf and mute man?

DISCUSSION: How do the people respond to Jesus?

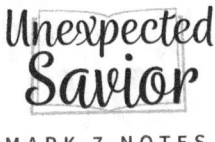

Unexpected Savior

MARK 7 NOTES

Unexpected Savior

MARK 7 NOTES

Unexpected Savior

MARK 7 NOTES

Unexpected Savior

HOW SHOULD I RESPOND?

Who is Jesus? What did He come to accomplish?

Write a prayer of thanksgiving for who He is.

Because God is:

    I can:

Unexpected Savior

TEACHING NOTES

Unexpected Savior

TEACHING NOTES

Unexpected Savior

GROUP NOTES

Unexpected Savior

GROUP NOTES

Unexpected Savior

MARK 8

READ MARK 8

WHAT DOES THIS SAY?

Write a 2–3 sentence summary of this passage.

Who? What? Where? When?

List any repeated words or phrases.

List any transitional words.

WHAT DOES THIS SAY ABOUT GOD?

What characteristics of God do you see in this passage?

WHAT DOES THIS MEAN?

Look up the following words in the dictionary and write out their definitions:

Leaven:

Christ/Messiah:

_____:

_____:

Unexpected
Savior

CROSS-REFERENCES

1 Corinthians 5:6–8:

Isaiah 9:6–7:

Jeremiah 23:5–6:

Colossians 3:1–17:

_____:

STARTER QUESTIONS

How does Mark show Jesus as a Man of Sorrows, Servant, or Savior in this passage?

In this chapter, what does Mark show that Jesus has authority over?

What are the similarities between the feeding of the four thousand and the feeding of the five thousand? What are the differences?

Unexpected Savior

MARK 8 NOTES

What is leaven? What does it do?

DISCUSSION: In this context, why is Jesus using leaven to warn His disciples about the Pharisees and Herod?

Again, who do people say Jesus is?

Who does Peter profess Jesus to be?

What does Jesus say in His rebuke of Peter?

DISCUSSION: How does Jesus describe what He came to do?

129

Unexpected Savior

DISCUSSION: What does it look like to follow Jesus?

How is this unexpected to the original audience?

DISCUSSION: How do we lay aside our own agendas and set our minds on the things of God?

Unexpected Savior

MARK 8 NOTES

Unexpected Savior

MARK 8 NOTES

Unexpected Savior

MARK 8 NOTES

HOW SHOULD I RESPOND?

Who is Jesus? What did He come to accomplish?

Write a prayer of thanksgiving for who He is.

Because God is:

I can:

Unexpected
Savior

TEACHING NOTES

Unexpected Savior

TEACHING NOTES

Unexpected Savior

GROUP NOTES

Unexpected Savior

GROUP NOTES

Unexpected Savior

MARK 9

READ MARK 9

WHAT DOES THIS SAY?

Write a 2–3 sentence summary of this passage.

Who? What? Where? When?

List any repeated words or phrases.

List any transitional words.

Unexpected Savior

MARK 9 NOTES

WHAT DOES THIS SAY ABOUT GOD?

What characteristics of God do you see in this passage?

WHAT DOES THIS MEAN?

Look up the following words in the dictionary and write out their definitions:

Transfigure:

Suffer:

_____:

_____:

141

CROSS-REFERENCES

Exodus 24:15–18:

Deuteronomy 18:15–22:

Romans 14:13–23:

_____ :

_____ :

STARTER QUESTIONS

How does Mark show Jesus as a Man of Sorrows, Servant, or Savior in this passage?

Reread Mark 1:9–11. Compare Jesus' baptism to Jesus' transfiguration.

142

Unexpected
Savior

DISCUSSION: What does God say about Jesus in Mark 9:7? How does this mark a shift in Mark's gospel?

What are the scribes doing with the disciples? How does this compare to what He just experienced on the mountain top?

What does Jesus say to the disciples in v. 19?

What does the father say to Jesus?

DISCUSSION: What does this teach us about our own unbelief?

How does Jesus describe the family of God in vv. 30–50?

DISCUSSION: How does Jesus model each of these?

DISCUSSION: How do these Old Testament verses add to your understanding of salt and the kingdom of God?

Exodus 30:34–38:

Leviticus 2:13:

Numbers 18:19:

2 Chronicles 13:5:

Ezekiel 43:24:

Unexpected Savior

MARK 9 NOTES

Unexpected Savior

MARK 9 NOTES

Unexpected Savior

MARK 9 NOTES

HOW SHOULD I RESPOND?

Who is Jesus? What did He come to accomplish?

Write a prayer of thanksgiving for who He is.

Because God is:

    I can:

Unexpected Savior

TEACHING NOTES

Unexpected
Savior

TEACHING NOTES

Unexpected
Savior

GROUP NOTES

Unexpected
Savior

GROUP NOTES

Unexpected Savior

MARK 10

READ MARK 10

WHAT DOES THIS SAY?

Write a 2–3 sentence summary of this passage.

Who? What? Where? When?

List any repeated words or phrases.

List any transitional words.

Unexpected Savior

WHAT DOES THIS SAY ABOUT GOD?

What characteristics of God do you see in this passage?

WHAT DOES THIS MEAN?

Look up the following words in the dictionary and write out their definitions:

Divorce:

Persecution:

_____:

_____:

Unexpected Savior

MARK 10 NOTES

CROSS-REFERENCES

Romans 7:1–6:

Psalm 52:

_____ :

_____ :

_____ :

STARTER QUESTIONS

How does Mark show Jesus as a Man of Sorrows, Servant, or Savior in this passage?

How does Jesus describe the family of God this passage?

156

DISCUSSION: How does Jesus model each of these?

How do these Old Testament passages give deeper understanding to vv. 1–12?

Isaiah 54:4–8:

Jeremiah 3:20:

Jeremiah 31:31–34:

What question do the disciples ask in v. 26?

How does Jesus respond?

DISCUSSION: What does this tell us about our salvation?

What do James and John request of Jesus? What does this tell us about their understanding of who Jesus is?

What name does Bartimaues call Jesus? What does this tell us about his understanding of who Jesus is?

Unexpected Savior

MARK 10 NOTES

Unexpected Savior

MARK 10 NOTES

160

Unexpected Savior

MARK 10 NOTES

Unexpected Savior

HOW SHOULD I RESPOND?

Who is Jesus? What did He come to accomplish?

Write a prayer of thanksgiving for who He is.

Because God is:

    I can:

Unexpected
Savior

TEACHING NOTES

Unexpected
Savior

TEACHING NOTES

Unexpected Savior

GROUP NOTES

Unexpected Savior

GROUP NOTES

Unexpected Savior

MARK 11

Unexpected
Savior

MARK 11 NOTES

READ MARK 11
WHAT DOES THIS SAY?

Write a 2–3 sentence summary of this passage.

Who? What? Where? When?

List any repeated words or phrases.

List any transitional words.

WHAT DOES THIS SAY ABOUT GOD?

What characteristics of God do you see in this passage?

WHAT DOES THIS MEAN?

Look up the following words in the dictionary and write out their definitions:

Prayer:

Temple Courts:

_____:

_____:

Unexpected
Savior

MARK 11 NOTES

CROSS-REFERENCES

1 Samuel 6:7–8:

Romans 2:1–11:

_____:

_____:

_____:

STARTER QUESTIONS

How does Mark show Jesus as a Man of Sorrows, Servant, or Savior in this passage?

Which Jewish festival is approaching?

How does this story show the fulfillment of the following Old Testament prophecies:

Zechariah 9:9–17:

170

Psalm 118 (with emphasis on vv. 25–26):

DISCUSSION: What is the theme of those two Old Testament passages? How does this confirm who Jesus is and what He came to do?

What story is found in the middle of the story of the fig tree? Given its placement, how does this explain the symbolism of the fig tree?

What does Jesus say the house of the Lord is called?

What have the religious leaders made it?

DISCUSSION: How do these quoted Old Testament passages help explain the meaning of vv. 15–25?

Isaiah 56:1–8:

Jeremiah 7:1–15:

DISCUSSION: As believers and Christ-followers, how do we live out Isaiah 56:1–8 so that we do not act as those in Jeremiah 7:1–15?

Unexpected Savior

MARK 11 NOTES

Unexpected
Savior

MARK 11 NOTES

174

Unexpected Savior

MARK 11 NOTES

Unexpected
Savior

HOW SHOULD I RESPOND?

Who is Jesus? What did He come to accomplish?

Write a prayer of thanksgiving for who He is.

Because God is:

    I can:

Unexpected Savior

TEACHING NOTES

Unexpected Savior

TEACHING NOTES

Unexpected Savior

GROUP NOTES

179

Unexpected
Savior

GROUP NOTES

Unexpected Savior

MARK 12

READ MARK 12

WHAT DOES THIS SAY?

Write a 2–3 sentence summary of this passage.

Who? What? Where? When?

List any repeated words or phrases.

List any transitional words.

Unexpected
Savior

WHAT DOES THIS SAY ABOUT GOD?

What characteristics of God do you see in this passage?

WHAT DOES THIS MEAN?

Look up the following words in the dictionary and write out their definitions:

Hypocrisy:

Condemnation:

_____:

_____:

CROSS-REFERENCES

Deuteronomy 6:4–6:

Leviticus 19:9–18:

_____:

_____:

_____:

STARTER QUESTIONS

How does Mark show Jesus as a Man of Sorrows, Servant, or Savior in this passage?

DISCUSSION: How do these cross-references help explain the parable in vv. 1–12?
  Psalm 118:

  Isaiah 5:1–7:

Unexpected
Savior

MARK 12 NOTES

Acts 4:5–12:

1 Peter 2:4–8:

DISCUSSION: How do vv. 13–44 reflect the meaning of the parable in vv. 1–12?

DISCUSSION: How do these cross-references help explain the meaning of vv. 28–40?
Hebrews 10:1–10:

Psalm 110:

How does Jesus describe the teachers, scribes, and rich people in vv. 38–44.

185

How does he describe the widow?

To whom does Jesus reveal the truth about the widow?

DISCUSSION: Looking at the chapter as a whole, what point is Mark making about who Jesus is and what it means to follow Him?

Unexpected Savior

MARK 12 NOTES

187

Unexpected Savior

MARK 12 NOTES

Unexpected Savior

MARK 12 NOTES

HOW SHOULD I RESPOND?

Who is Jesus? What did He come to accomplish?

Write a prayer of thanksgiving for who He is.

Because God is:

    I can:

190

Unexpected
Savior

TEACHING NOTES

Unexpected Savior

TEACHING NOTES

Unexpected Savior

GROUP NOTES

193

Unexpected Savior

GROUP NOTES

Unexpected Savior

MARK 13

Unexpected
Savior

READ MARK 13

WHAT DOES THIS SAY?

Write a 2–3 sentence summary of this passage.

Who? What? Where? When?

List any repeated words or phrases.

List any transitional words.

WHAT DOES THIS SAY ABOUT GOD?

What characteristics of God do you see in this passage?

WHAT DOES THIS MEAN?

Look up the following words in the dictionary and write out their definitions:

Guard:

Abomination:

Desolation:

_____:

Unexpected
Savior

CROSS-REFERENCES

Deuteronomy 13:1–5:

Psalm 105:43:

Isaiah 40:8:

_____:

_____:

STARTER QUESTIONS

How does Mark show Jesus as a Man of Sorrows, Servant, or Savior in this passage?

DISCUSSION: How do these cross-references help explain this passage?

Daniel 11:29–35:

Hebrews 12:18–29:

Romans 8:18–25:

In vv. 24–25, Jesus quotes Isaiah 13:10 and 34:4. Read these Old Testament prophecies in context. What parallels do you see to Mark 13?

In v. 26, Jesus alludes to Daniel 7:13–18. What truth is Jesus revealing about Himself? How does this passage give the disciples (and us) hope?

DISCUSSION: What two actions does Jesus repeatedly tell His disciples to take in Mark 13?

DISCUSSION: Read 1 Thessalonians 5:1–11. Practically, how do we take these actions?

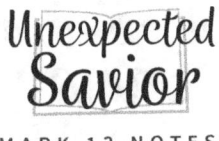

Unexpected Savior

MARK 13 NOTES

Unexpected Savior

MARK 13 NOTES

Unexpected Savior

HOW SHOULD I RESPOND?

Who is Jesus? What did He come to accomplish?

Write a prayer of thanksgiving for who He is.

Because God is:

    I can:

Unexpected Savior

TEACHING NOTES

Unexpected
Savior

TEACHING NOTES

Unexpected Savior

GROUP NOTES

207

Unexpected Savior

GROUP NOTES

Unexpected Savior

MARK 14

Unexpected
Savior

READ MARK 14

WHAT DOES THIS SAY?

Write a 2–3 sentence summary of this passage.

Who? What? Where? When?

List any repeated words or phrases.

List any transitional words.

WHAT DOES THIS SAY ABOUT GOD?

What characteristics of God do you see in this passage?

WHAT DOES THIS MEAN?

Look up the following words in the dictionary and write out their definitions:

Sorrow:

Betray:

_____:

_____:

Unexpected
Savior

CROSS-REFERENCES

Deuteronomy 15:11:

Psalm 110:1:

Daniel 7:13–14:

_____:

_____:

STARTER QUESTIONS

How does Mark show Jesus as a Man of Sorrows, Servant, or Savior in this passage?

Write out a timeline of the events of Mark 14 and where each took place.

Unexpected
Savior

MARK 14 NOTES

How much was the flask of ointment worth?

What happens right after the anointing in Mark's account?

DISCUSSION: How is this woman's response to Jesus different than Judas' response?

DISCUSSION: Read Exodus 12:1–28. What parallels do you see to Mark 14?

DISCUSSION: Read Isaiah 53. What parallels do you see to Mark 14?

DISCUSSION: How do we see these Old Testament passages fulfilled in these stories?

Deuteronomy 16:1–8:

Unexpected Savior

2 Kings 9:6:

Zechariah 13:7:

Psalm 41:9:

Proverbs 27:6:

Unexpected Savior

MARK 14 NOTES

Unexpected Savior

MARK 14 NOTES

Unexpected Savior

MARK 14 NOTES

HOW SHOULD I RESPOND?

Who is Jesus? What did He come to accomplish?

Write a prayer of thanksgiving for who He is.

Because God is:

I can:

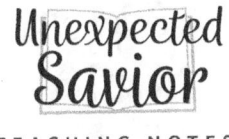

Unexpected Savior

TEACHING NOTES

Unexpected Savior

TEACHING NOTES

Unexpected Savior

GROUP NOTES

Unexpected Savior

GROUP NOTES

Unexpected Savior

MARK 15

READ MARK 15

<u>**WHAT DOES THIS SAY?**</u>

Write a 2–3 sentence summary of this passage.

Who? What? Where? When?

List any repeated words or phrases.

List any transitional words.

WHAT DOES THIS SAY ABOUT GOD?

What characteristics of God do you see in this passage?

WHAT DOES THIS MEAN?

Look up the following words in the dictionary and write out their definitions:

Compelled/Forced:

Battalion:

_____:

_____:

Unexpected Savior

CROSS-REFERENCES

Acts 3:11–16:

_____:

_____:

_____:

_____:

STARTER QUESTIONS

How does Mark show Jesus as a Man of Sorrows, Servant, or Savior in this passage?

Write out a timeline of the events of Mark 15 and where each took place.

Unexpected Savior

MARK 15 NOTES

DISCUSSION: Read Isaiah 53 again. What parallels do you see to Mark 15?

DISCUSSION: Read Psalm 22. What parallels do you see to Mark 15?

DISCUSSION: How do we see these Old Testament passages fulfilled in these stories?

Amos 8:9:

Psalm 69:21:

Proverbs 31:6–7:

Psalm 109:25:

227

Psalm 38:11:

Write out v. 38.

Read Hebrews 10:19–25. What can we now do because of the sacrifice of Jesus?

Set aside time to re-read Mark 15, giving yourself space to contemplate what Jesus endured. Then, write a prayer of thanksgiving for the cross and what was accomplished on our behalf.

Unexpected Savior

MARK 15 NOTES

Unexpected Savior

MARK 15 NOTES

Unexpected Savior

MARK 15 NOTES

HOW SHOULD I RESPOND?

Who is Jesus? What did He come to accomplish?

Write a prayer of thanksgiving for who He is.

Because God is:

    I can:

232

Unexpected Savior

TEACHING NOTES

Unexpected Savior

TEACHING NOTES

Unexpected Savior

GROUP NOTES

Unexpected Savior

GROUP NOTES

Unexpected Savior

MARK 16

READ MARK 16

WHAT DOES THIS SAY?

Write a 2–3 sentence summary of this passage.

Who? What? Where? When?

List any repeated words or phrases.

List any transitional words.

Unexpected
Savior

WHAT DOES THIS SAY ABOUT GOD?

What characteristics of God do you see in this passage?

WHAT DOES THIS MEAN?

Look up the following words in the dictionary and write out their definitions:

Resurrection:

_____ :

_____ :

_____ :

Unexpected
Savior

CROSS-REFERENCES

1 Timothy 3:16:

Hebrews 1:

Philippians 2:1–11:

_____:

STARTER QUESTIONS

How does Mark show Jesus as a Man of Sorrows, Servant, or Savior in this passage?

Who were the first to know about Jesus' resurrection?

What did the angel tell them?

Unexpected Savior

MARK 16 NOTES

DISCUSSION: How did they respond? Remembering the context of Mark, why do you think Mark ends his gospel this way? (Note: vv. 9–20 do not appear in the earliest manuscripts of Mark and most consider v. 8 the end of his gospel.)

DISCUSSION: After studying the gospel of Mark, who do you say Jesus is?

DISCUSSION: What have you learned about God through Mark?

DISCUSSION: How has studying Mark changed you and your faith?

Unexpected Savior

MARK 16 NOTES

Unexpected Savior

MARK 16 NOTES

Unexpected Savior

MARK 16 NOTES

Unexpected
Savior

MARK 16 NOTES

HOW SHOULD I RESPOND?

Who is Jesus? What did He come to accomplish?

Write a prayer of thanksgiving for who He is.

Because God is:

    I can:

246

Unexpected
Savior

TEACHING NOTES

Unexpected
Savior

TEACHING NOTES

Unexpected Savior

GROUP NOTES

Unexpected
Savior

GROUP NOTES

Unexpected Savior

ADDITIONAL NOTES

ADDITIONAL NOTES

252

Unexpected
Savior

ADDITIONAL NOTES

Unexpected Savior

ADDITIONAL NOTES

feasting at the table

Chicken is a dinnertime staple in our house, and I'm constantly looking for new ways to make boring, bland chicken breasts taste amazing and tender. To make chicken flavorful usually requires marinating it for hours, and there's nothing more frustrating than realizing at five o'clock that you forgot to marinate chicken for dinner.

That's why I love this simple and flavorful one-skillet meal. It is quick and doesn't require much prep work.

A cast iron skillet is the secret to this dish. No other pan can replicate the flavor cast iron yields. The seasoning from the skillet as well as the spices sprinkled on the chicken give this dish its flavor. I keep a well-stocked spice bin and love to build my own spice mixes. But if that's not your thing, you can use taco or fajita seasoning. Toasting the rice in the butter for a minute before adding the broth gives the rice a nutty depth of flavor. I like to control the amount of salt I cook with, so I use low-sodium broth and no salt added tomatoes. You may need to adjust the salt based on the ingredients you use. I also hand-crush the tomatoes a little more when adding them to the pan. Lastly, finishing this dish in the oven infuses the chicken with moisture and perfectly cooks the rice.

Top your dish with your favorite taco toppings: avocado, cheese, sour cream, fresh tomatoes, shredded lettuce—whatever strikes your fancy! Voila! You have a quick, simple, and flavorful chicken dish that is sure to be a crowd pleaser! Enjoy!

255

SKILLET MEXICAN CHICKEN AND RICE

Time: 30 minutes
Yield: Serves 4–6

INGREDIENTS
Seasoning Mix:
1 teaspoon salt
1 teaspoon chili powder
½ teaspoon cumin
¼ teaspoon onion
¼ teaspoon garlic
¼ teaspoon paprika

4 chicken breasts, cut in half

2 tablespoons butter
1½ cups rice
2¼ cups low-sodium vegetable or chicken broth
1 cup crushed or diced fire-roasted tomatoes (preferably no salt added)
1 teaspoon salt

INSTRUCTIONS
1. Place the oven rack in the middle of the oven and preheat the oven to 425 degrees.
2. Preheat a large cast iron skillet over medium-high heat.
3. Sprinkle half of the seasoning mix on one side of the chicken.
4. Place half of the chicken seasoning side down in the hot skillet and cook for 2–3 minutes. While browning, sprinkle seasoning on the other side of the chicken. Flip the chicken and brown the other side. Remove the chicken from the skillet and place on a plate. Repeat with the second half of the chicken. (It will not be fully cooked.)
5. With all the chicken set aside on the plate, add the butter to the skillet. Once melted, add the rice and stir to coat the rice in butter, letting it toast for 1–2 minutes.
6. Add the broth, tomatoes, and salt. Stir and bring to a boil.
7. Once boiling, add the chicken back in.
8. Carefully (and using oven mitts!), move the skillet to the oven. Bake for 15 minutes.
9. Serve with your favorite taco toppings.

about Erin

ERIN H. WARREN is passionate about equipping and encouraging women to discover God's truths for themselves. She is the author of *Feasting on Truth: Savor the Life-giving Word of God*, leads and teaches Bible study through her ministry Feasting on Truth, and has published several Bible studies. She and her husband, Kris, have three littles (who aren't so little anymore), and they live in Central Florida. She loves a house full of people and a table full of food and hopes tacos never go out of style. You can find more information about Feasting on Truth on her website: FeastingOnTruth.com. You can also connect with her on Instagram: @erinhwarren and @feastingontruth and YouTube: www.youtube.com/c/erinhwarren.

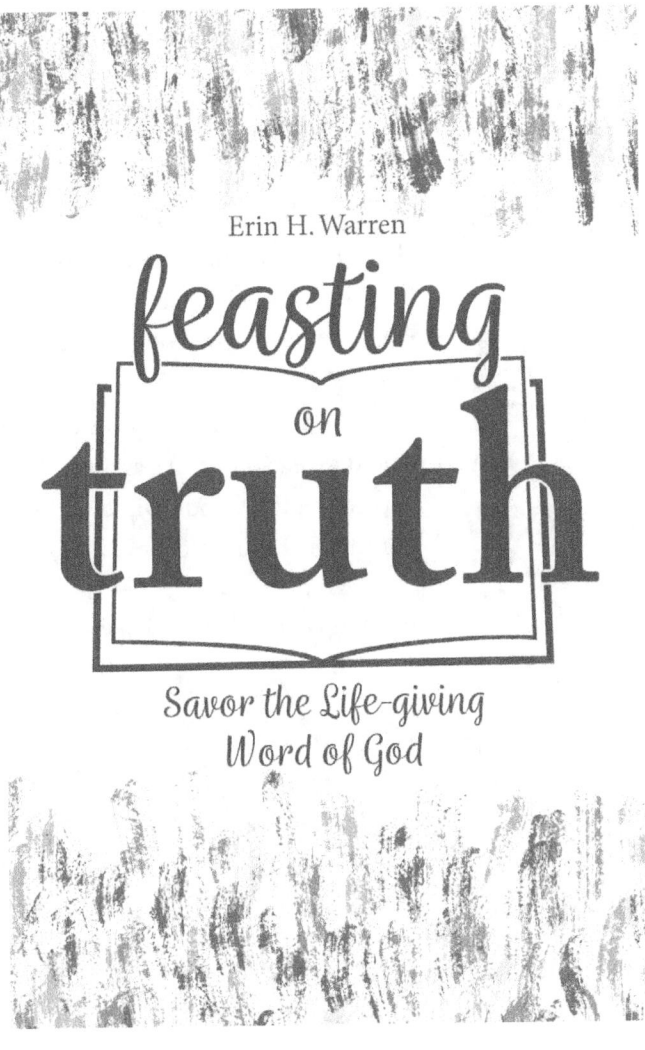

Erin H. Warren

feasting on truth

Savor the Life-giving Word of God

FEASTING ON TRUTH

SAVOR THE LIFE-GIVING WORD OF GOD

The Word of God is our very life, but Erin Warren felt anything but alive. Her husband was sick. Her world was falling apart, and she had questions. Feel-good faith was not enough; she needed deep, sustaining truths.

Through her own wrestling, Erin Warren addresses the obstacles that held her back when it came to Bible study and how she discovered to savor the life-giving Word of God.

The word *feast* is rooted in abundance. That is what awaits us in the pages of Scripture: a table laid out before us, not only for our essential nourishment, but for our enjoyment.

FeastingOnTruth.com/Books

TO DWELL IN OUR MIDST

A STUDY OF THE TABERNACLE AND HOW IT POINTS US TO JESUS

Why study this ancient tent? What does knowing about the Tabernacle have to do with our faith on this side of the cross? Everything. This tent is not merely ritual or history or good information—it's essential to understanding our salvation. Our detailed and deliberate God gave us the Tabernacle because one day, He would give us Jesus. It's an invitation into a relationship with our Holy God. Discover God's plan to dwell in our midst through Jesus Christ.

FeastingOnTruth.com/Dwell

STORIES FROM THE WILDERNESS

A STUDY OF THE ISRAELITES' JOURNEY FROM EGYPT TO THE PROMISED LAND

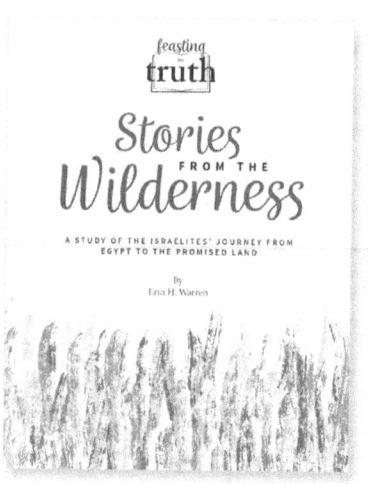

The wilderness. It is a place that feels hard, empty, lifeless, and pathless, and it often leaves us with questions about who God is. But where we see a place that is worthless, confusing, and chaotic, God sees a place to display His power. Time and time again throughout Scripture, God takes the worthless, seemingly wasteful, confusing, chaotic, and empty places and uses them as a backdrop to prove His character, draw us in, and display His glory.

FeastingOnTruth.com/Wilderness

WAYMAKER

AN ADVENT STUDY THROUGH THE BOOK OF HEBREWS

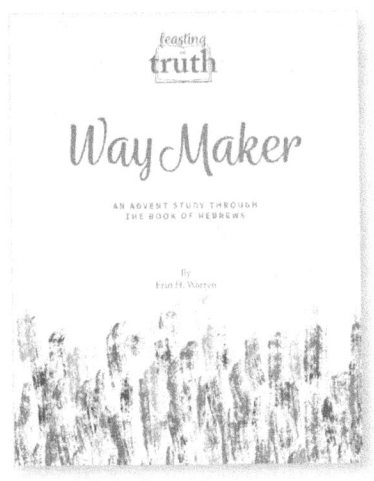

Jesus' coming was more than giving us forgiveness of sins or to part the way before us. He came to part the divide between God and us, between us and heaven. Jesus is the One who made a way to a restored relationship with God. No other book gives us a more comprehensive view of Jesus as our Way Maker than the book of Hebrews.

FeastingOnTruth.com/WayMaker

LIGHT & LIFE

AN INDUCTIVE STUDY ON PSALM 119

We hear it all the time: we need to read the Bible every day. But why is it so important that we know, understand, and apply this ancient book to our lives today? What's in it for us? In Psalm 119, we see over and over that God's Word brings life, and it's a light to guide us. If we truly knew the power the Word of God has in our lives, we wouldn't be able to put it down.

FeastingOnTruth.com/LightAndLife

BY HIS GRACE FOR HIS GLORY

AN INDUCTIVE STUDY ON THE BOOK OF ROMANS

Romans is foundational yet deep. It's hard to understand yet simple. It is an incredibly powerful book that has been changing lives for centuries, and the truths in these sixteen chapters have the power to change our faith too. There are many familiar verses in Romans, and we associate this book with evangelism. But it is so much more! Discover what it looks like to live by His grace for His glory.

FeastingOnTruth.com/Romans

www.ingramcontent.com/pod-product-compliance
Lightning Source LLC
Chambersburg PA
CBHW081325120626
46546CB00011B/3219